EMPOWERING MANTRAS
FOR AWESOME WOMEN

EMPOWERING MANTRAS

FOR AWESOME WOMEN

CICO BOOKS

LONDON NEW YORK

Published in 2018 by CICO Books
An imprint of Ryland Peters & Small Ltd
20–21 Jockey's Fields   341 E 116th St
London WC1R 4BW   New York, NY 10029

www.rylandpeters.com

10 9 8 7 6 5 4 3 2 1

Design © CICO Books 2018

For photography credits, see pages 143–144.

The author's moral rights have been asserted.
All rights reserved. No part of this publication
may be reproduced, stored in a retrieval system,
or transmitted in any form or by any means,
electronic, mechanical, photocopying, or otherwise,
without the prior permission of the publisher.

A CIP catalog record for this book is available from
the Library of Congress and the British Library.

ISBN: 978-1-78249-566-6

Printed in China

Designer: Paul Tilby
Commissioning editor: Kristine Pidkameny
Senior editor: Carmel Edmonds
Art director: Sally Powell
Production manager: Gordana Simakovic
Publishing manager: Penny Craig
Publisher: Cindy Richards

INTRODUCTION

This brilliant collection of wise and powerful words is a must-have for any 21st-century woman. Whether you want a reminder of your worth, a boost towards smashing boundaries and glass ceilings, or simply a hit of positivity, you'll find your inspiration here.

Among motivational mantras to shift your mind-set, you'll also discover the sage words of women who shaped history—from abolitionists Harriet Beecher Stowe and Harriet Tubman and suffragist Elizabeth Cady Stanton to novelists such as Charlotte Brontë and Jane Austen and poets such as Emily Dickinson and Christina Rossetti.

You might like to choose a mantra or quotation each morning and keep it in your mind as you face the day's challenges. Try copying words that have particularly resonated with you into your journal, or pin them up around your home or workplace to inspire you. You could even send your favorite words to a friend to help her find her inner strength.

Remember: you are the heroine of your life.

HERE'S TO STRONG WOMEN. MAY WE KNOW THEM. MAY WE BE THEM. MAY WE RAISE THEM

FIND
THE
WONDER
WOMAN
INSIDE
YOU

YOUR MIND HAS THE POWER AND YOUR HEART WILL FIND THE WAY

BEAUTY BEGINS THE MOMENT YOU DECIDE TO BE YOURSELF.

Coco Chanel

KNOW THE VALUE OF KNOWING YOUR VALUE

INHALE
CONFIDENCE,
EXHALE
DOUBT

LITTLE GIRLS
WITH DREAMS
BECOME WOMEN
WITH VISION

HEAR

ME

ROAR

DIAMONDS

**ADVENTURES
ARE FOREVER**

**NEXT TO TRYING
AND WINNING,
THE BEST THING IS
TRYING AND FAILING.**

L.M. Montgomery

NEVERTHELESS, SHE PERSISTED

REMEMBER YOU ARE ADORED

BE FEARLESS
TAKE
ACTION

I AM
AT HOME
IN MY
PERSONAL
STORY

YOU HAVE WITHIN YOU
THE STRENGTH, THE PATIENCE,
AND THE PASSION TO REACH FOR THE
STARS TO CHANGE THE WORLD.

Harriet Tubman

STEP
INTO YOUR
POWER

UNHOOK FROM PRAISE AND CRITICISM

BE YOUR OWN BEST FRIEND

CHOOSE COURAGE OVER COMPROMISE

ARE YOU IN?

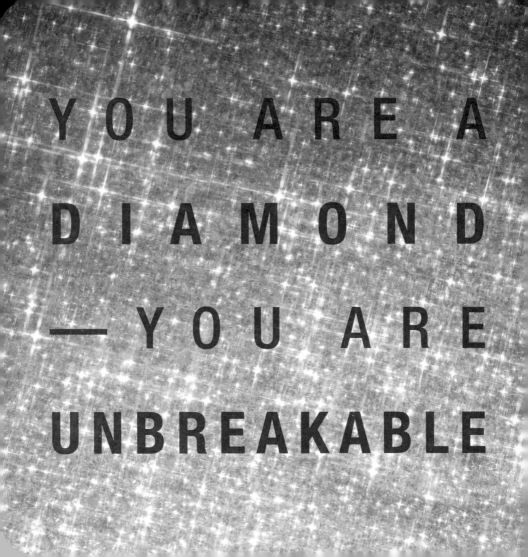

BE DARING

MY WOMAN IS TO STAND ALONE, AND HELP HERSELF... STRONG-MINDED, STRONG-HEARTED, STRONG-SOULED, AND STRONG-BODIED.

Louisa May Alcott

LET GO OF EXPECTATIONS AND STAY CURIOUS

WHERE ATTENTION GOES
ENERGY FLOWS

YOU HAVE AN APPOINTMENT WITH LIFE

COME INTO FULL VIEW

IF YOU LOOK THE RIGHT WAY,
YOU CAN SEE THAT THE WHOLE
WORLD IS A GARDEN.

Frances Hodgson Burnett

THERE IS A STUBBORNNESS ABOUT ME
THAT NEVER CAN BEAR TO BE FRIGHTENED
AT THE WILL OF OTHERS. MY COURAGE ALWAYS RISES
AT EVERY ATTEMPT TO INTIMIDATE ME.

Jane Austen

ONE CANNOT CONSENT TO CREEP WHEN ONE HAS AN IMPULSE TO SOAR.

Helen Keller

DO
WHAT
YOU
LOVE

**NO ONE
CAN MAKE
YOU FEEL
INFERIOR
WITHOUT
YOUR
CONSENT**

Eleanor Roosevelt

THE BEST PROTECTION ANY WOMAN CAN HAVE ... IS COURAGE.

Elizabeth Cady Stanton

STOP
WISHING.
START
DOING

I AM NO BIRD; AND NO NET ENSNARES ME; I AM A FREE HUMAN BEING WITH AN INDEPENDENT WILL.

Charlotte Brontë

WOMEN ARE THE REAL ARCHITECTS
OF SOCIETY.

Harriet Beecher Stowe

TRUST YOUR INTUITION

SPEAK THROUGH YOUR LIFE.
YOU WILL CHANGE LIVES

I WANT TO SING LIKE BIRDS SING. NOT WORRY
WHO LISTENS OR WHAT THEY THINK.

Rumi

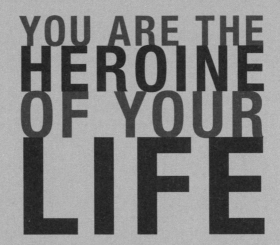

THE MOST EFFECTIVE WAY TO DO IT, IS TO DO IT.

Amelia Earhart

I DO NOT WISH WOMEN TO
HAVE POWER OVER MEN;
BUT OVER THEMSELVES.

Mary Wollstonecraft

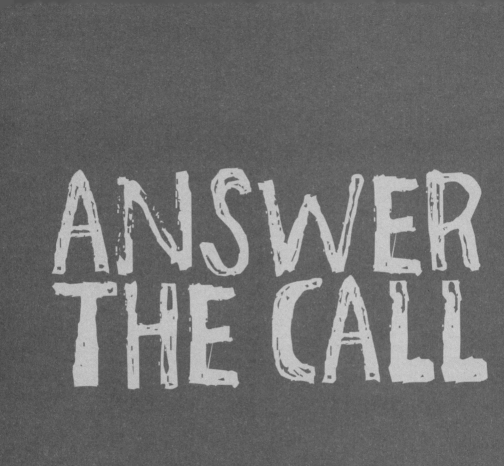

BE YOUR OWN KIND OF BEAUTIFUL

I ALLOW SHE HAS SMALL CLAIMS
TO PERFECTION; BUT THEN,
I MAINTAIN THAT, IF SHE WERE
MORE PERFECT, SHE WOULD BE
LESS INTERESTING.

Anne Brontë

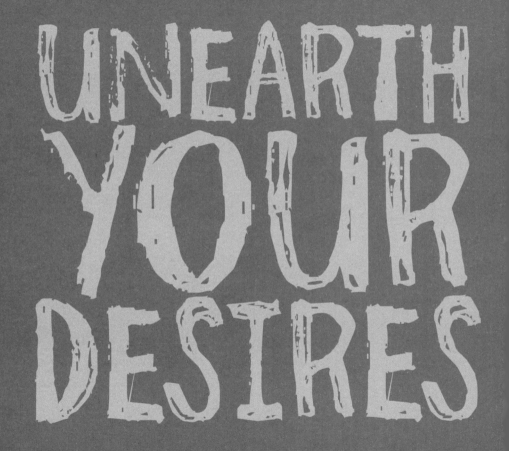

I HATE TO HEAR YOU TALKING AS IF
WOMEN WERE ALL FINE LADIES,
INSTEAD OF RATIONAL CREATURES.
WE NONE OF US EXPECT TO BE
IN SMOOTH WATER ALL OUR DAYS.

Jane Austen

DON'T WAIT FOR SOMEONE TO GIVE YOU PERMISSION

THE BEGINNING IS ALWAYS TODAY

Mary Shelley

I WOULD ALWAYS RATHER BE
HAPPY THAN DIGNIFIED.

Charlotte Brontë

FOR THERE IS NO FRIEND LIKE A SISTER
IN CALM OR STORMY WEATHER;
TO CHEER ONE ON THE TEDIOUS WAY,
TO FETCH ONE IF ONE GOES ASTRAY,
TO LIFT ONE IF ONE TOTTERS DOWN,
TO STRENGTHEN WHILST ONE STANDS.

Christina Rossetti

IN THE WAVES OF CHANGE, WE FIND OUR TRUE DIRECTION

DO WHAT THEY THINK YOU CAN'T DO

DON'T
STOP
UNTIL
YOU'RE
PROUD

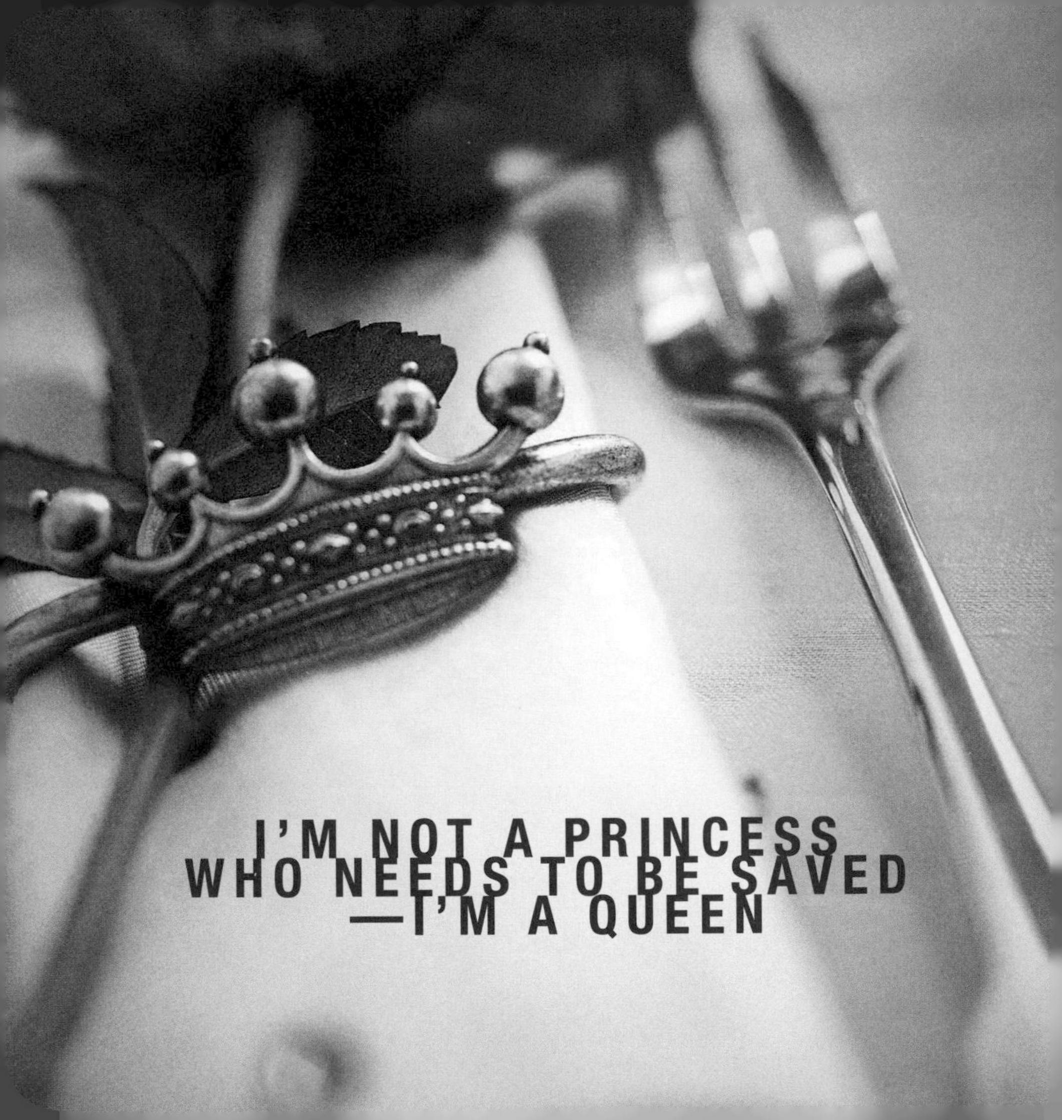
I'M NOT A PRINCESS
WHO NEEDS TO BE SAVED
—I'M A QUEEN

THE
FUTURE
IS
FEMALE

AND THOUGH SHE BE BUT LITTLE, SHE IS FIERCE

William Shakespeare

I CONNECT
WITH
MY
TRUE
SELF

WHAT TRULY MATTERS?

AND, OF COURSE, MEN KNOW BEST
ABOUT EVERYTHING, EXCEPT WHAT
WOMEN KNOW BETTER.

George Eliot

PUT ON YOUR LIPSTICK AND FACE THE DAY

DARE TO BE
YOUR OWN
ILLUMINATION

WE KNOW
WHAT
WE
ARE,
BUT KNOW,
NOT WHAT
WE MAY BE

William Shakespeare

I AM NOT AN ANGEL, AND I WILL NOT
BE ONE TILL I DIE: I WILL BE MYSELF.

Charlotte Brontë

I AM NOT
AFRAID;
I WAS
BORN
TO DO THIS.

Joan of Arc

TRUTH IS POWERFUL AND IT PREVAILS.

Sojourner Truth

I MATTER EQUALLY

YOU ARE ASTONISHING

INVITE THE MAGIC IN

IT IS NOT EASY
TO BE A
PIONEER
—BUT OH, IT IS
FASCINATING!

Elizabeth Blackwell

DON'T SAY
"I CAN'T DO IT."

SAY "I CAN'T
DO IT YET."

WHAT'S YOUR SUPERPOWER?

EMPOWERED
WOMEN
EMPOWER
WOMEN

THE POWER IS IN YOUR HANDS

I'M NOT AFRAID OF STORMS,
FOR I'M LEARNING
HOW TO SAIL MY SHIP.

Louisa May Alcott

WE NEVER KNOW HOW HIGH WE ARE
TILL WE ARE CALLED TO RISE;
AND THEN, IF WE ARE TRUE TO PLAN,
OUR STATURES TOUCH THE SKIES.

Emily Dickinson

PROVE
THEM
WRONG

YOU
ARE
GOOD
ENOUGH

SELF-CONFIDENCE

IS THE

BEST OUTFIT

**MAKE NO APOLOGIES
FOR WHO YOU ARE**

AT FIRST PEOPLE REFUSE TO BELIEVE
THAT A STRANGE NEW THING CAN BE
DONE, THEN THEY BEGIN TO HOPE IT
CAN BE DONE, THEN THEY SEE IT CAN BE
DONE—THEN IT IS DONE AND ALL THE
WORLD WONDERS WHY IT WAS NOT
DONE CENTURIES AGO.

Frances Hodgson Burnett

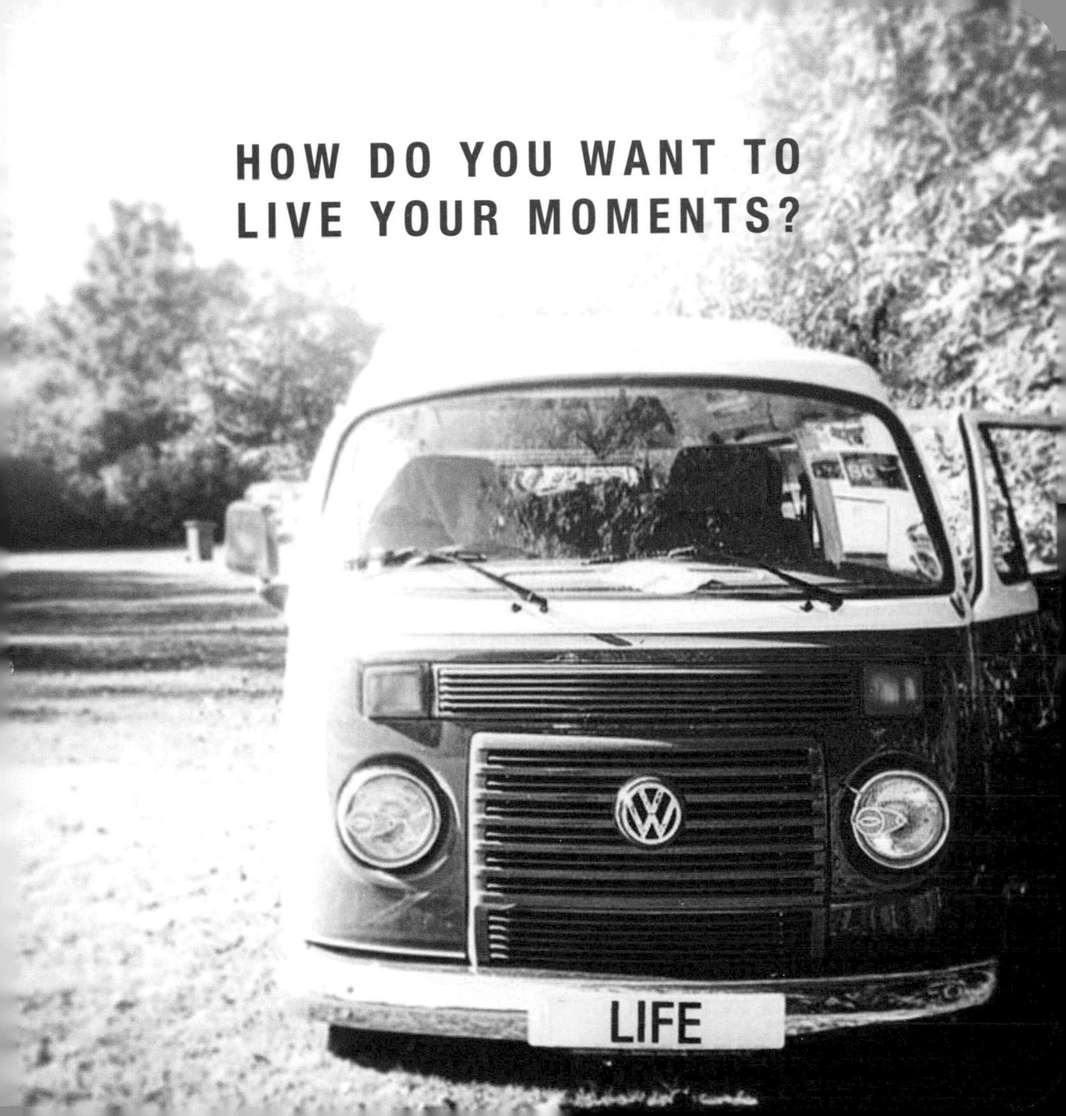
HOW DO YOU WANT TO
LIVE YOUR MOMENTS?
LIFE

I AM STRONG
I AM POWERFUL
I AM A WOMAN

PHOTOGRAPHY CREDITS

KEY: *ph* = photographer

Front cover © Getty/courtneyk

Back cover © 123rf.com/mtkang

Page 1 © Getty/STUDIO BOX

Page 2 © Ryland Peters and Small/Victoria Smith editor sfgirlbybay.com. *ph* Rachel Whiting

Page 3 © Getty/Matt Champlin

Page 4 © Getty/Lumina Imaging

Page 7 © Ryland Peters and Small/*ph* Chris Everard

Page 8 © Ryland Peters and Small/*ph* Tom Leighton

Page 10 © Ryland Peters and Small/Clare Nash's house in London. *ph* Polly Wreford

Page 11 © Ryland Peters and Small/Jon Pellicoro Artist and Designer. *ph* Winfried Heinze

Page 13 © Ryland Peters and Small/*ph* Polly Wreford

Page 14 © CICO Books/ ph Emma Mitchell

Page 15 © Ryland Peters and Small/*ph* Chris Everard

Page 17 © CICO Books/ *ph* Joanna Henderson

Page 19 © Getty/Catherine MacBride

Page 21 © Getty/Daniel Kulinski

Page 22 © Getty/PeopleImages

Page 25 © Ryland Peters and Small/Victoria Smith editor sfgirlbybay.com. *ph* Rachel Whiting

Page 26 © Getty/Matt Champlin

Page 29 © Ryland Peters and Small/The home of the interior decorator Caroline Van Thillo in Belgium. *ph* Polly Wreford

Page 30 © CICO Books/ *ph* Joanna Henderson

Page 32 © CICO Books/ *ph* Penny Wincer

Page 35 © Getty/STUDIO BOX

Page 36 © CICO Books/ *ph* Mark Lohman

Page 39 © Ryland Peters and Small/*ph* Chris Everard

Page 41 © Emma Kirkby: follow her on Instagram @emmaloukirkby

Page 42 © Megan Winter-Barker: follow her on Instagram @megwinterbarker

Page 43 © Lena Karlsson: follow her on Instagram @asakapop or check out her website: www.asakapop.com

Page 44 © Getty/Lumina Imaging

Page 45 © Ryland Peters and Small/The home of fashion designer Virginie Denny & painter Alfonso Vallès. *ph* Debi Treloar

Page 47 © Getty/Corey Jenkins

Page 49 © Ryland Peters and Small/*ph* Chris Everard

Page 50 © Getty/humonia

Page 51 © Ryland Peters and Small/*ph* Hans Blomquist

Page 52 © Ryland Peters and Small/The London home of Tracey Boyd and Adrian Wright. *ph* Debi Treloar

Page 53 © Ryland Peters and Small/The home of the artist Lou Kenlock, Oxfordshire. *ph* Catherine Gratwicke

Page 54 © Ryland Peters and Small/*ph* Francesca Yorke

Page 56 © Getty/Naufal MQ

Page 57 © CICO Books/ *ph* Caroline Arber

Page 58 © Ryland Peters and Small/*ph* Kate Whitaker

Page 60 © Getty/Gregor Schuster

Page 63 © Getty/Christopher Fanelli/EyeEm

Page 64 © Ryland Peters and Small/*ph* Daniel Farmer

Page 66 © Getty/Henn Photography

Page 69 © Emma Kirkby: follow her on Instagram @emmaloukirkby

Page 70 © Ryland Peters and Small/*ph* Paul Massey

Page 71 © Megan Winter-Barker: follow her on Instagram @megwinterbarker

Page 73 © Lena Karlsson: follow her on Instagram @asakapop or check out her website: www.asakapop.com

Page 74 © Ryland Peters and Small/Philip & Catherine Mould's house in Oxfordshire. *ph* Chris Tubbs

Page 75 © CICO Books/ *ph* Caroline Arber

Page 77 © Getty/Arman Zhenikeyev

Page 79 © Ryland Peters and Small/*ph* Debi Treloar

Page 81 © Getty/Erik Isakson

Page 83 © CICO Books/ *ph* Geoff Dann

Page 84 © CICO Books/ *ph* Martin Norris

Page 85 © Getty/Alistair Berg

Page 87 © CICO Books/ *ph* Emma Mitchell

Page 88 © Ryland Peters and Small/*ph* Dan Duchars

Page 91 © Emma Kirkby: follow her on Instagram @emmaloukirkby

Page 92 © Ryland Peters and Small/The home of Ida Susanne Collier of sukkertoyforoyet.blogspot.no. *ph* Catherine Gratwicke

Page 93 © Ryland Peters and Small/*ph* Chris Everard

Page 94 © Lena Karlsson: follow her on Instagram @asakapop or check out her website: www.asakapop.com

Page 95 © Lena Karlsson: follow her on Instagram @asakapop or check out her website: www.asakapop.com

Page 96 © Ryland Peters and Small/*ph* Sandra Lane

Page 98 © Megan Winter-Barker: follow her on Instagram @megwinterbarker

Page 99 © Getty/Manuela

Page 100 © Emma Kirkby: follow her on Instagram @emmaloukirkby

Page 102 © Ryland Peters and Small/*ph* David Brittain

Page 103 © Getty/Zheka-Boss

Page 105 © Lena Karlsson: follow her on Instagram @asakapop or check out her website: www.asakapop.com

Page 106 © Lena Karlsson: follow her on Instagram @asakapop or check out her website: www.asakapop.com

Page 109 © Ryland Peters and Small/*ph* Debi Treloar

Page 111 © Ryland Peters and Small/*ph* Winfried Heinze

Page 112 © Ryland Peters and Small/Wim and Josephine's apartment in Amsterdam. *ph* Debi Treloar

Page 115 © Emma Kirkby: follow her on Instagram @emmaloukirkby

Page 116 © Ryland Peters and Small/The home of Nils Tunebjer in Sweden. *ph* Paul Ryan

Page 119 © Emma Kirkby: follow her on Instagram @emmaloukirkby

Page 121 © Ryland Peters and Small/*ph* Martin Brigdale

Page 123 © Getty/Classen Rafael/ EyeEm

Page 125 © Getty/FatCamera

Page 126 © Getty/Donald Iain Smith

Page 127 © Ryland Peters and Small/The home of the decorator Bunny Turner of www.turnerpocock.co.uk. *ph* Polly Wreford

Page 129 © Getty/Kristina Kokhanova

Page 131 © Getty/The_ Chickenwing

Page 132 © Getty/Marc Romanelli

Page 135 © Getty/Klaus Vedfelt

Page 137 © Getty/Lori Andrews

Page 139 © Getty/Corey Jenkins

Page 141 © Megan Winter-Barker: follow her on Instagram @megwinterbarker

Page 142 © Getty/Manuel Breva Colmeiro